📖 READERS

Level 1

A Day at Greenhill Farm
Truck Trouble
Tale of a Tadpole
Surprise Puppy!
Duckling Days
A Day at Seagull Beach
Whatever the Weather
Busy Buzzy Bee
Big Machines
Wild Baby Animals
A Bed for the Winter
Born to be a Butterfly
Dinosaur's Day
Feeding Time
Diving Dolphin
Rockets and Spaceships
My Cat's Secret
First Day at Gymnastics
A Trip to the Zoo
I Can Swim!
A Trip to the Library
A Trip to the Doctor
A Trip to the Dentist
I Want To Be A Ballerina
Animal Hide and Seek

Submarines and Submersibles
Animals at Home
Let's Play Football
Homes Around the World
LEGO: Trouble at the Bridge
LEGO: Secret at Dolphin Bay
Star Wars: What is a Wookiee?
Star Wars: Ready, Set, Podrace!
Star Wars: Luke Skywalker's Amazing Story
Star Wars Clone Wars: Watch Out
    for Jabba the Hutt!
Star Wars Clone Wars: Pirates... and Worse!
Power Rangers Jungle Fury: We are
    the Power Rangers
A Day in the Life of a Builder
A Day in the Life of a Dancer
A Day in the Life of a Firefighter
A Day in the Life of a Teacher
A Day in the Life of a Musician
A Day in the Life of a Doctor
A Day in the Life of a Police Officer
A Day in the Life of a TV Reporter
Gigantes de Hierro *en español*
Crías del mundo animal *en español*
Indiana Jones: Indy's Adventures

Level 2

Dinosaur Dinners
Fire Fighter!
Bugs! Bugs! Bugs!
Slinky, Scaly Snakes!
Animal Hospital
The Little Ballerina
Munching, Crunching, Sniffing, and Snooping
The Secret Life of Trees
Winking, Blinking, Wiggling, and Waggling
Astronaut: Living in Space
Twisters!
Holiday! Celebration Days around the World
The Story of Pocahontas
Horse Show
Survivors: The Night the Titanic Sank
Eruption! The Story of Volcanoes
The Story of Columbus
Journey of a Humpback Whale
Amazing Buildings
Feathers, Flippers, and Feet
Outback Adventure: Australian Vacation
Sniffles, Sneezes, Hiccups, and Coughs
Ice Skating Stars
Let's Go Riding
I Want to Be a Gymnast
Starry Sky

Earth Smart: How to Take Care
    of the Environment
Water Everywhere
Telling Time
A Trip to the Theater
Journey of a Pioneer
LEGO: Castle Under Attack
LEGO: Rocket Rescue
Star Wars: Journey Through Space
Star Wars: A Queen's Diary
Star Wars: R2-D2 and Friends
Star Wars Clone Wars: Anakin in Action!
Star Wars: Jedi in Training
Star Wars Clone Wars: Beware of Bounty
    Hunters!
MLB: A Batboy's Day
MLB: Let's Go to the Ballpark!
Spider-Man: Worst Enemies
Meet the X-Men
¡Insectos! *en español*
¡Bomberos! *en español*
La Historia de Pocahontas *en español*
Indiana Jones: Traps and Snares
Inauguration Day
WWE: Jeff Hardy
WWE: John Cena

A Note to Parents

DK READERS is a compelling program for beginning readers, designed in conjunction with leading literacy experts, including Dr. Linda Gambrell, Distinguished Professor of Education at Clemson University. Dr. Gambrell has served as President of the National Reading Conference, the College Reading Association, and the International Reading Association.

Beautiful illustrations and superb full-color photographs combine with engaging, easy-to-read stories to offer a fresh approach to each subject in the series. Each DK READER is guaranteed to capture a child's interest while developing his or her reading skills, general knowledge, and love of reading.

The five levels of DK READERS are aimed at different reading abilities, enabling you to choose the books that are exactly right for your child:

Pre-level 1: Learning to read
Level 1: Beginning to read
Level 2: Beginning to read alone
Level 3: Reading alone
Level 4: Proficient readers

The "normal" age at which a child begins to read can be anywhere from three to eight years old. Adult participation through the lower levels is very helpful for providing encouragement, discussing storylines, and sounding out unfamiliar words.

No matter which level you select, you can be sure that you are helping your child learn to read, then read to learn!

LONDON, NEW YORK, MUNICH,
MELBOURNE, and DELHI

Project Editor Deborah Murrell
Art Editor Catherine Goldsmith
US Editor Regina Kahney
Production Sean Daly
Picture Researcher Frances Vargo
Picture Librarian Sally Hamilton
Jacket Designer Natalie Godwin
Publishing Manager Bridget Giles

Reading Consultant
Linda Gambrell, Ph.D.

First American edition, 2000
This edition, 2009
09 10 11 12 13 10 9 8 7 6 5 4 3 2 1
Published in the United States by DK Publishing
375 Hudson Street, New York, New York 10014

Published in Great Britain by Dorling Kindersley Limited

DK books are available at special discounts when purchased
in bulk for sales promotions, premiums,
fund-raising, or educational use.
For details, contact: DK Publishing Special Markets
375 Hudson Street, New York, New York 10014
SpecialSales@dk.com

A catalog record for this book is available
from the Library of Congress

ISBN: 978-0-7566-5585-3 (pb)
ISBN: 978-0-7566-5594-5 (plc)

Color reproduction by Colourscan, Singapore
Printed and bound in China by L. Rex Printing Co. Ltd

The publisher would like to thank the following for
their kind permission to reproduce their images:
Photography: Dave King, John Downs 14
Illustrations: Simone Boni/L.R. Galante
Natural History Museum: 8-9, 11, 12-13, 14, 15, 21
Ardea London Ltd.: Arthur Hayward 16-17
Jacket images: DK Images: Graham High at Centaur Studios
- modelmaker cb; Rough Guides (background)

All other images © Dorling Kindersley
For further information see www.dkimages.com

Discover more at
www.dk.com

DK READERS

Dinosaur's Day

Written by Ruth Thomson

DK Publishing

I am Triceratops.

I am a dinosaur.

I am big and strong.

Triceratops
(try-SER-uh-tops)

I have three spiky horns
on my head.
I have a bony frill
on my neck.

frill

I look fierce,
but I am gentle.

beak

I spend all day eating plants.
I snip off twigs and leaves
with my hard beak.

I live in a group
called a herd.
We keep watch
for fierce dinosaurs.
They might want to eat us!

All sorts of other dinosaurs
live near the river with us.

Everything is peaceful.

All of a sudden,
what do I see?

A Tyrannosaurus!
He is the fiercest dinosaur of all.

Tyrannosaurus
(tie-RAN-uh-SORE-us)

He has strong toes
and sharp claws.
He has a huge mouth
full of sharp teeth.

toes

A herd of light-footed dinosaurs
spots Tyrannosaurus too.
They run away on their long legs
as fast as they can.
They hide in the forest.

Ornithomimus
(OR-ni-thoh-MEE-mus)

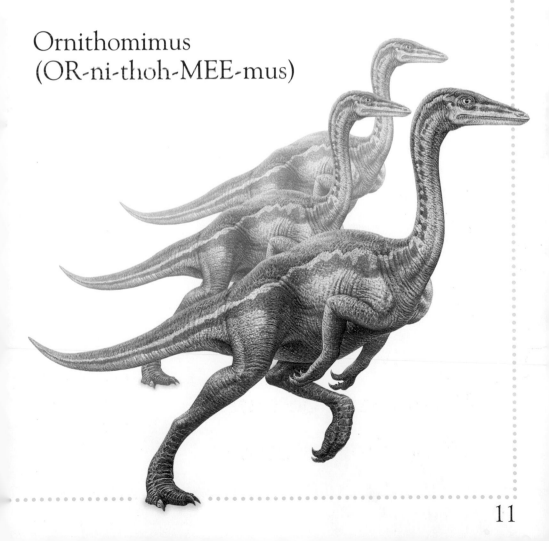

The duck-billed dinosaurs
stop eating.
They watch Tyrannosaurus.
If he comes too close,
they will run away.

bill

Edmontosaurus
(ed-MON-tuh-SORE-us)

The bone-headed dinosaur
looks up and sniffs the air.
He can smell Tyrannosaurus.
If Tyrannosaurus
comes too close,
he will run away too.

Pachycephalosaurus
(PAK-ee-SEF-uh-low-SORE-us)

The dinosaurs with head crests
hoot in alarm.

Parasaurolophus
(par-uh-sore-OLL-uh-fuss)

crest

The armored dinosaur has a club
on the end of his tail.
He gets ready to swing it
at Tyrannosaurus.

club

Ankylosaurus
(an-KIE-luh-SORE-us)

I am busy watching
all the other dinosaurs.
I forget to stay with my herd.

I can see Tyrannosaurus.

He can see me.

Tyrannosaurus runs towards me.

He looks hungry.

His eyes are glinting.

teeth

His mouth is open.

I can see his sharp teeth.

Thud!
Thud!

He comes nearer
and nearer.

21

Tyrannosaurus
stands up.
He is very tall.
He lifts his head
and roars loudly.

Tyrannosaurus is trying
to scare me,
but I am not scared.
I have my sharp horns
for fighting.
I have my bony frill
to protect me.

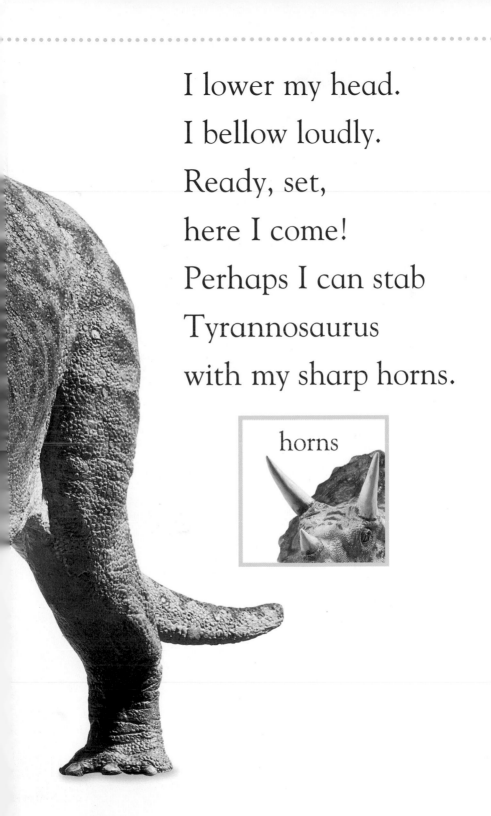

I lower my head.
I bellow loudly.
Ready, set,
here I come!
Perhaps I can stab
Tyrannosaurus
with my sharp horns.

horns

Tyrannosaurus tries to bite me
with his sharp teeth.
I am still not scared.
I kick up the dust.
I try to stab him.

Tyrannosaurus is getting tired.
He stops fighting and turns away.
He goes to look for
a smaller dinosaur
for his dinner.

Now I am safe.

I am going to look for my herd.

I am very hungry
after all that fighting.

I am glad to be back
with my herd
by the river.

The other dinosaurs
come back to the river as well.
They eat peacefully.

I hope Tyrannosaurus
won't come back again.

Picture word list

frill

page 5

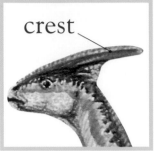
crest

page 15

beak

page 6

club

page 17

toes

page 10

teeth

page 20

bill

page 13

horns

page 25

Index